VIOLA
97VA

PRIMO ENCORES

Elementary-Level Ensembles
A Companion to ALL FOR STRINGS, Books 1 & 2

by Robert S. Frost

The Collection

PRIMO ENCORES is a collection of folk songs, classical themes, rounds, and original compositions arranged in such a way as to be extremely versatile in meeting the needs of the beginning level string orchestra. Each instrument has the melody line as well as additional harmony lines. By using all the parts a string orchestra is achieved. With the addition of piano, any size string class can successfully perform these selections.

Contents

1. Chopsticks 2
2. Who Comes Laughing 3
3. Polly Wolly Doodle 4
4. Pizzicadough 5
5. Grandfather's Clock 6
6. Carnival of Venice 7
7. Billy Boy 10
8. Turkey in the Straw 11
9. Merry Widow Waltz 12
10. Granite Rock 14
11. Welcome, Lovely May 15
12. Arkansas Traveler 16
13. Pomp and Circumstance 17
14. Sleeping Beauty Waltz 18
15. White Coral Bells 19
16. Trumpet Voluntary 20
17. Winter is Past 21
18. A Capital Ship 22
19. Struttin' 24

PRIMO ENCORES is available for Violin (97VN), Viola (97VA), Cello (97CO), String Bass (97SB), Piano Accompaniment (97PA), and Conductor Score (97F).

ISBN 0-8497-3382-0

© 1998 **Neil A. Kjos Music Company**, 4380 Jutland Drive, San Diego, California, 92117.
International copyright secured. All rights reserved. Printed in U.S.A.
WARNING! The contents of this publication are protected by copyright law. To copy or reproduce them by any method is an infringement of the copyright law. Anyone who reproduces copyrighted matter is subject to substantial penalties and assessments for each infringement.

1. Chopsticks

Traditional

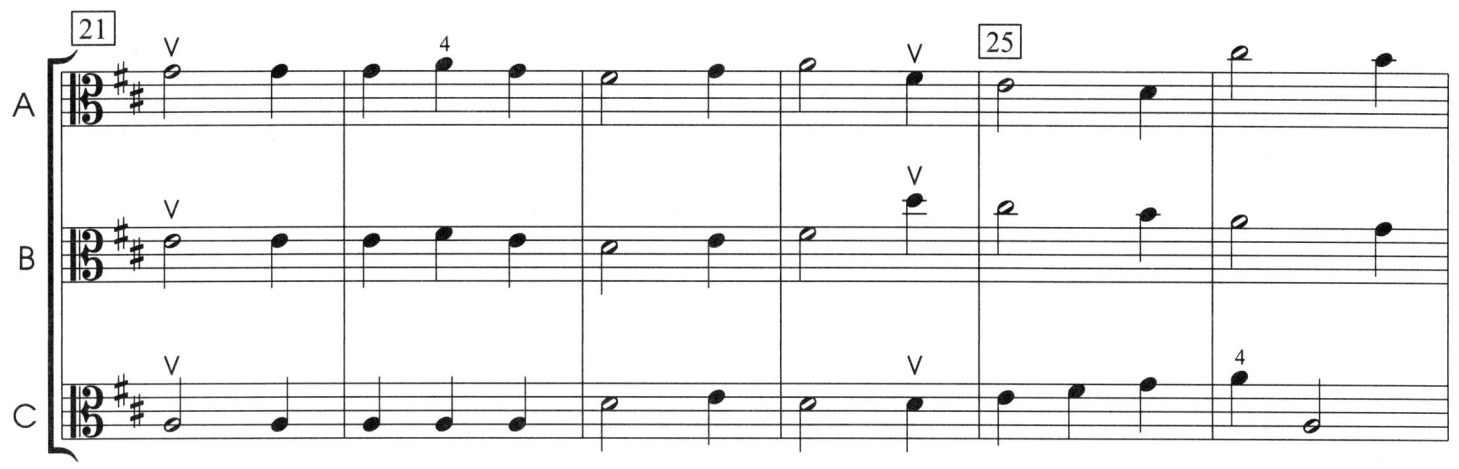

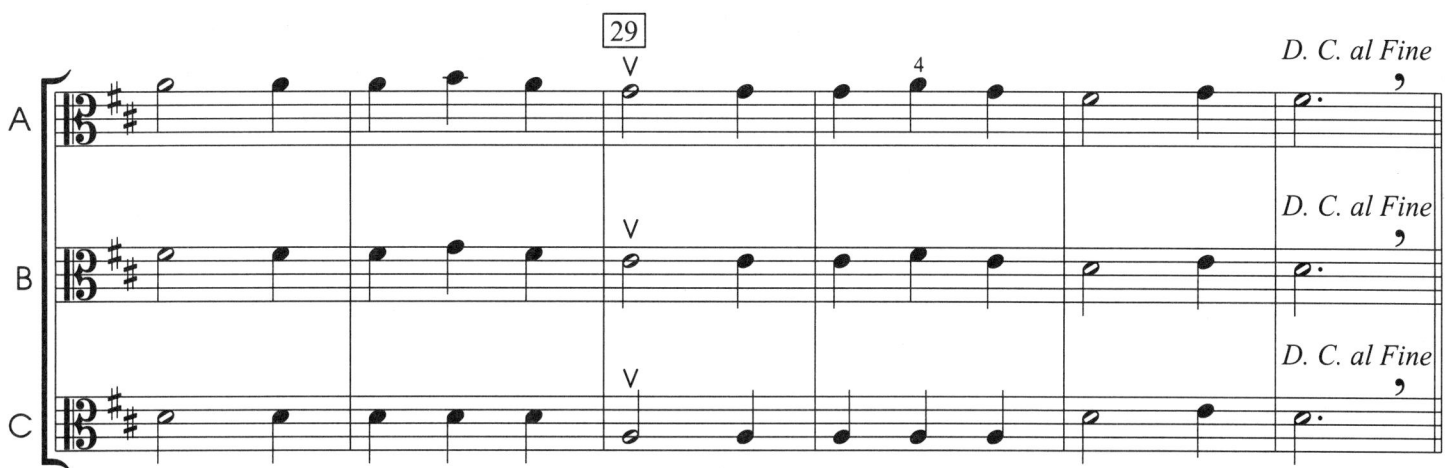

2. Who Comes Laughing

Round

3. Polly Wolly Doodle

American Folk Song

4. Pizzicadough

Robert S. Frost

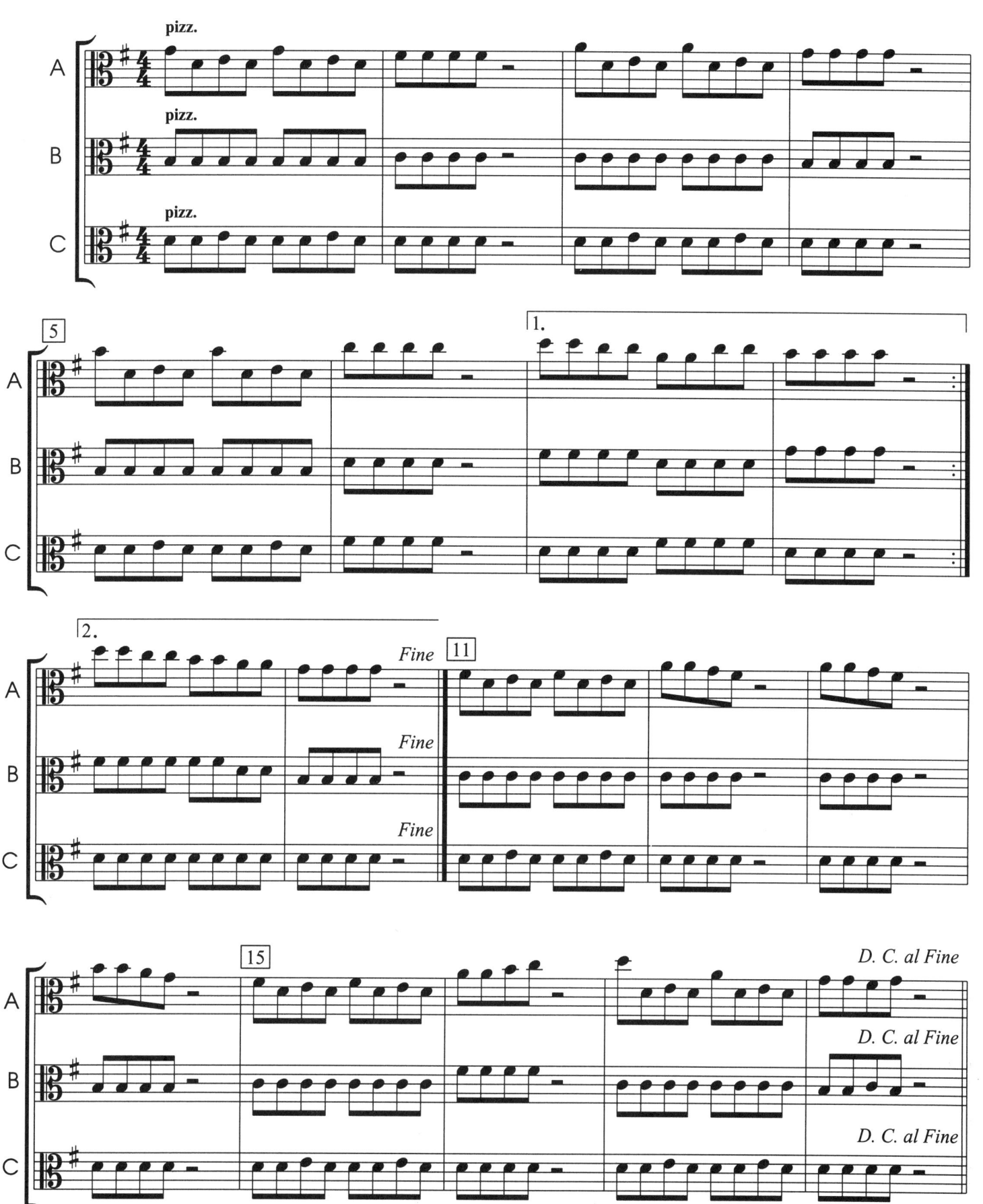

© 1998 Neil A. Kjos Music Company, 4380 Jutland Drive, San Diego, California, 92117.

97VA

5. Grandfather's Clock

Henry C. Work

6. Carnival of Venice

Nicolò Paganini

© 1998 Neil A. Kjos Music Company, 4380 Jutland Drive, San Diego, California, 92117.

7. Billy Boy

American Folk Song

8. Turkey in the Straw

American Fiddle Song

© 1998 Neil A. Kjos Music Company, 4380 Jutland Drive, San Diego, California, 92117.

9. Merry Widow Waltz

Franz Lehár

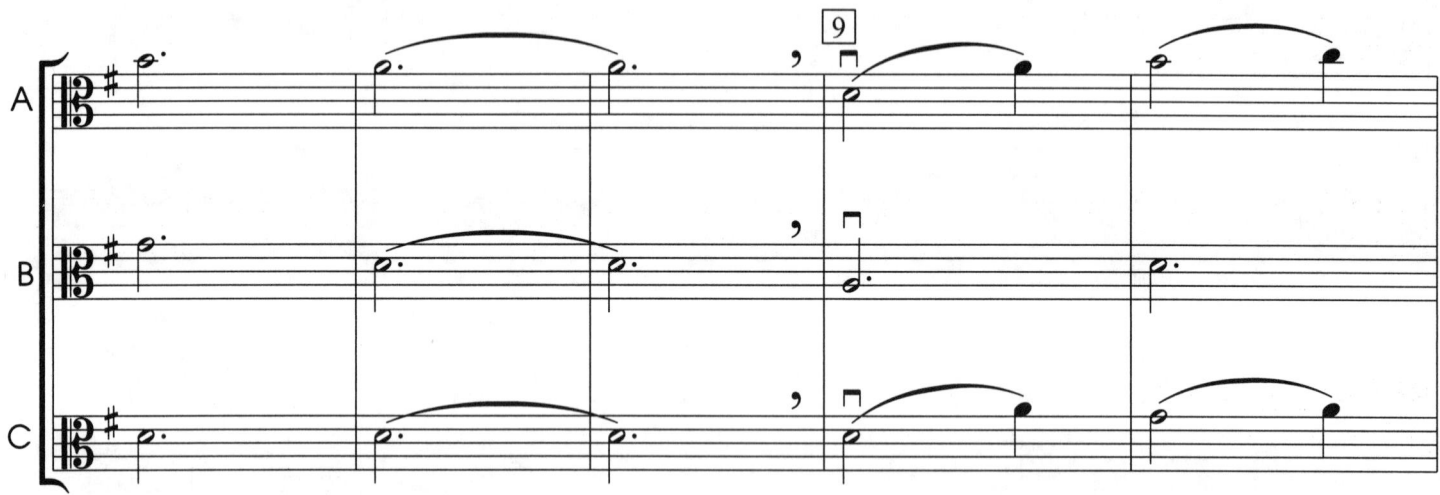
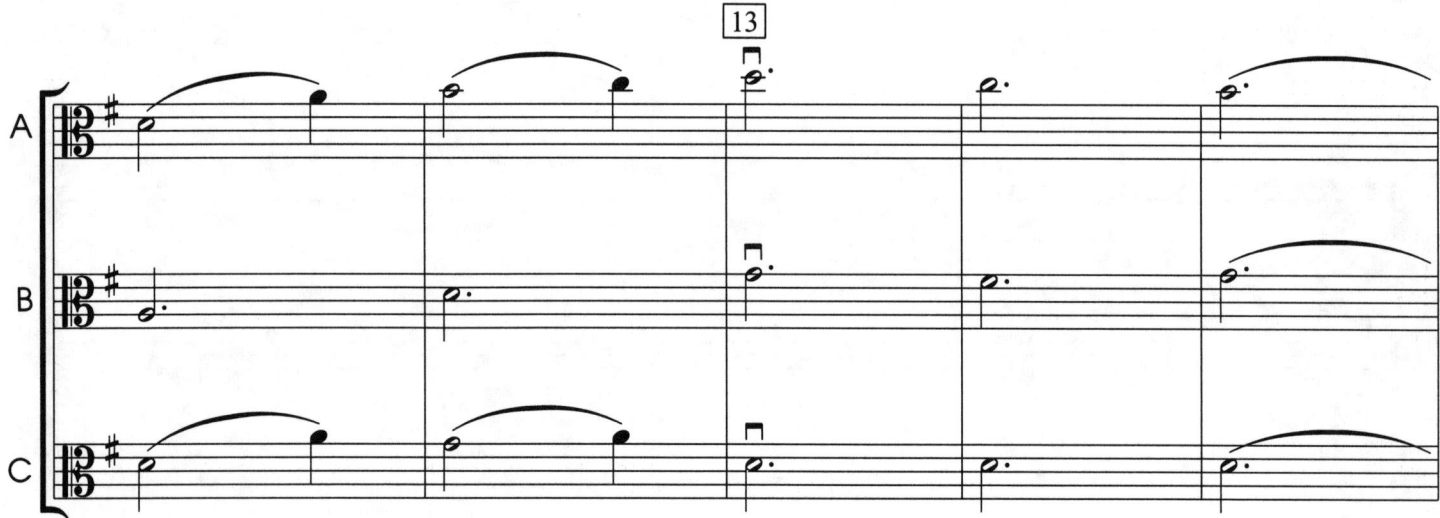

© 1998 Neil A. Kjos Music Company, 4380 Jutland Drive, San Diego, California, 92117.

10. Granite Rock

Robert S. Frost

11. Welcome, Lovely May

Franz Schubert - Round

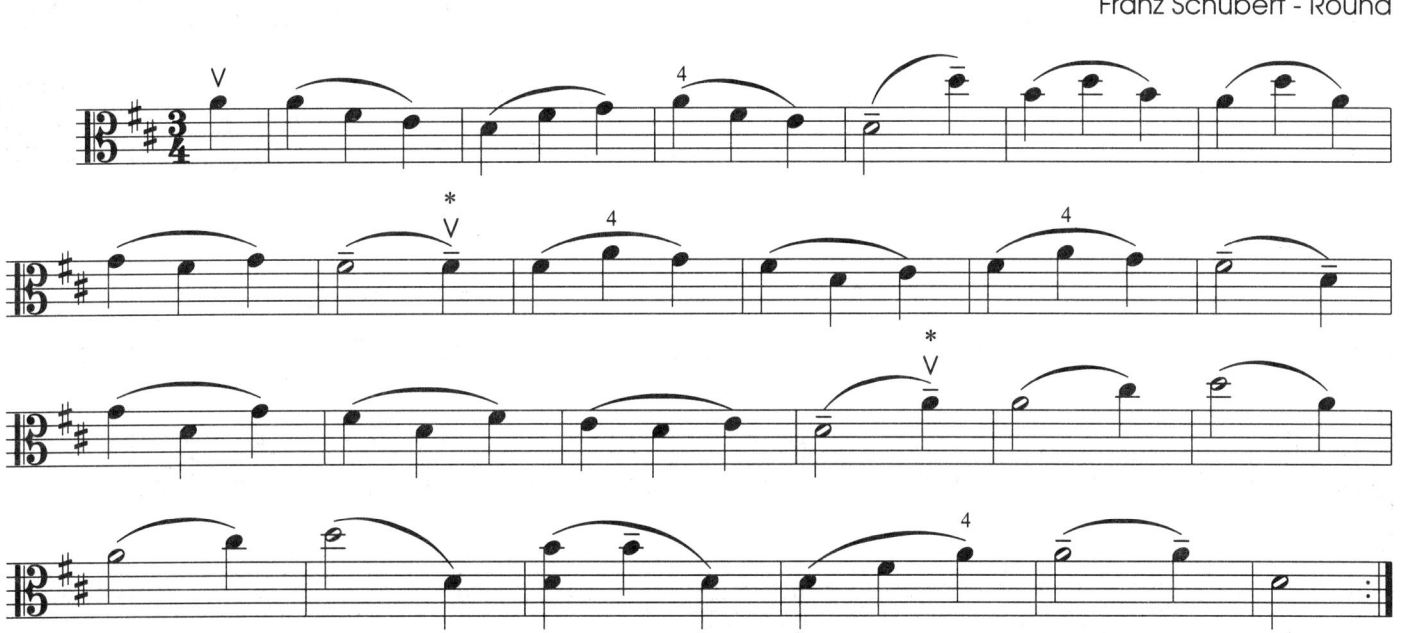

© 1998 Neil A. Kjos Music Company, 4380 Jutland Drive, San Diego, California, 92117.

12. Arkansas Traveler

American Fiddle Song

© 1998 Neil A. Kjos Music Company, 4380 Jutland Drive, San Diego, California, 92117.

13. Pomp and Circumstance

Edward Elgar

14. Sleeping Beauty Waltz

Peter I. Tchaikovsky

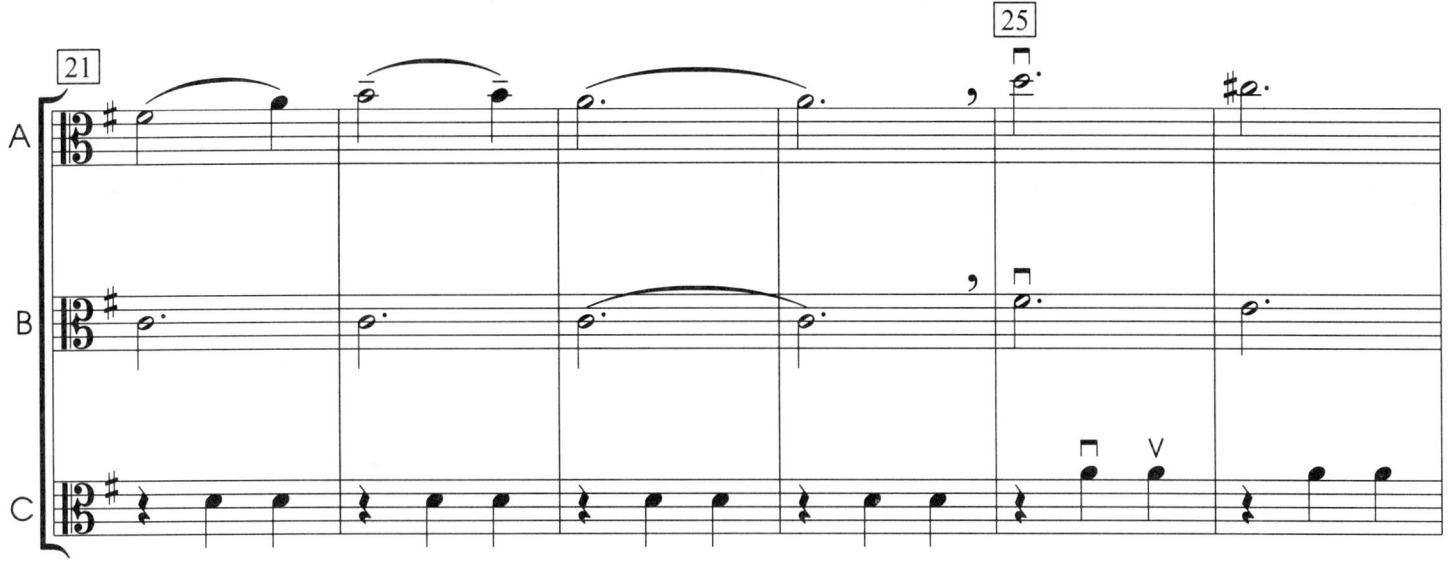

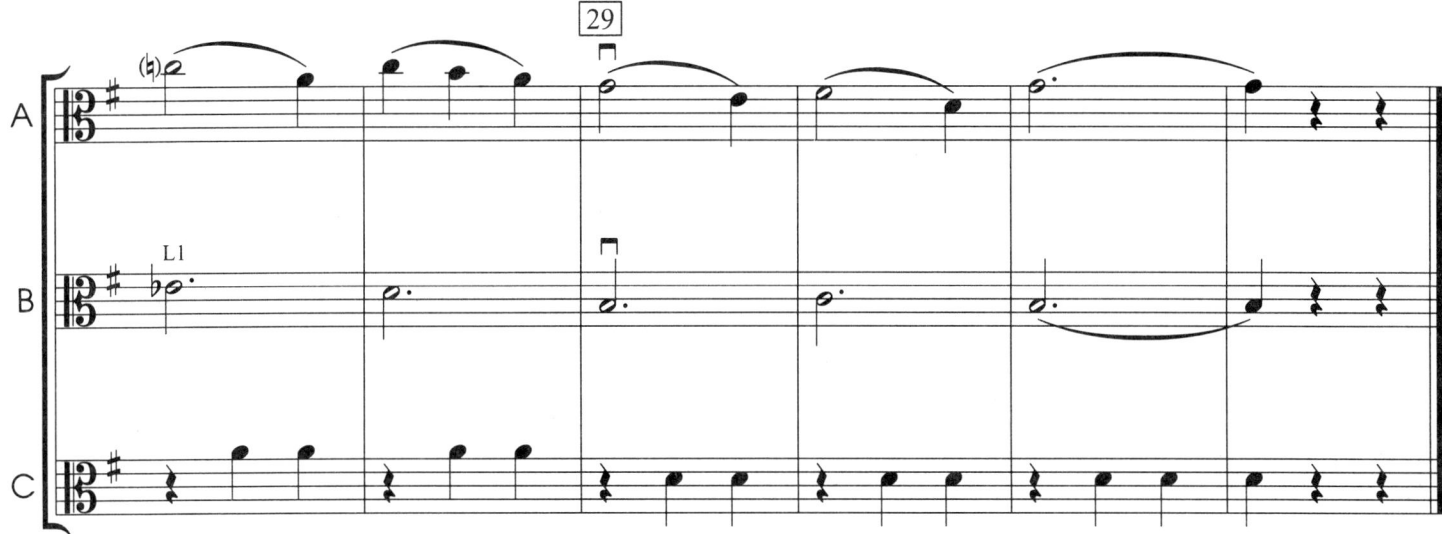

15. White Coral Bells

16. Trumpet Voluntary

Jeremiah Clarke

© 1998 Neil A. Kjos Music Company, 4380 Jutland Drive, San Diego, California, 92117.

17. Winter is Past

German-Round

18. A Capital Ship

English Folk Song

19. Struttin'

Robert S. Frost